ADVANCED EDUCATION.

THE RELATIONS OF THE NATIONAL AND STATE GOVERNMENTS TO ADVANCED EDUCATION.

BY

ANDREW D. WHITE.

A Paper read before the National Educational Association, at Detroit, Aug. 5, 1874.

BOSTON:
OFFICE OF OLD AND NEW,
143 WASHINGTON STREET.

THE TRADE SUPPLIED BY
F. B. PERKINS, BUSINESS AGENT.
LONDON: SAMPSON LOW & CO., 188 FLEET STREET.

1874.

Rev. James Martineau, L.L.D., the distinguished metaphysician and theologian, has engaged to furnish exclusively to "OLD AND NEW" a series of papers on

"The Transient and Permanent in Religion."

THE SUBJECTS ARE:

GOD IN NATURE.

GOD IN HUMANITY.

GOD IN HISTORY.

THE CHURCH AND ITS PRETENSIOUS CLAIMS.

THE PROTESTANT THEORY OF AUTHORITY.

THE HUMAN AND THE DIVINE ELEMENTS IN HISTORY.

THE HISTORICAL CHRIST.

RELIGION; NATURAL, REVEALED AND APOCALYPTIC.

THE MESSIANIC APOCALYPSE.

THE PAULINE AND JOHANNINE DOCTRINE OF CHRIST'S PERSON.

THE SENSE OF SIN AND THE DOCTRINES OF REDEMPTION.

THE SACRAMENTAL SUPERSTITION.

Readers who wish, can subscribe for the whole series, sent to one address, for $4.00.

OFFICE OF OLD AND NEW,

No. 143 Washington Street, Boston.

Stokes Gift 8-3-60

J. B. Angell

LC 173 .W52

THE RELATIONS

OF THE

NATIONAL AND STATE GOVERNMENTS

TO

ADVANCED EDUCATION.

A Paper read before the National Educational Association at Detroit, Aug. 5, 1874.

By ANDREW D. WHITE,

PRESIDENT OF CORNELL UNIVERSITY.

Reprinted from the October Number of Old and New.

[This address, which was read at Detroit, attracted the attention and cordial thanks of the large assembly there of gentlemen connected with public education. The body of men who are engaged in State universities, in normal schools, and other institutions supported by States, is now considerable. These men do not care to be set aside by an epigram, as being the mere tools of political parties, and as of no account except as political make-weights. They were, therefore, especially glad to hear a defence of public education in the higher walks of education.

On the other hand, the address, even as partially reported, has been challenged almost, of course, by the sectarian journals. For these reasons we are glad to publish, for consideration now and for preservation, from the author's manuscript, a much fuller report than any which has yet appeared. The demand for it among all persons interested in the subject is so large, that this special edition is reprinted in pamphlet form. — Eds. Old and New.]

Among all the modern nations, two stand pre-eminent for faith in public education, and for energy in providing it.

Of these, I name first the German nation. In the midst of great calamities and trials, and long years of hard work, and under administrations economical to parsimony, she has developed a system, which, for half a century, has won the admiration of the world by its intellectual triumphs, and which, in the past ten years, has aroused the world's wonder by its political and social triumphs.

Next I name the United States, where, in sight of all mankind, popular education is lifting a nation above all the efforts of demagogues in the field, in the senate-house, and in the press.

In one thing these two nations have adopted the same policy, and obtained the same results. Each has made abundant provision for primary and secondary education in public schools, and both have found in this a source of triumphs both in peace and war, which have placed them in the foremost rank among modern nations.

But in the other half of the system, — in provision for advanced education, in high scientific and industrial schools and universities, — they have followed courses directly opposite, and with directly opposite results.

Germany has carried out her fundamental principle logically. Having started with the idea that the people of a nation should provide for the education of the nation, it has stopped at no imaginary line: it has provided for the education of the whole people, — for the young, in primary and secondary schools; for those more advanced, in technical schools and universities. The result is now before the world.

Forth from these institutions have come a majority of the greatest leaders of modern thought and practice, — not only great theologians and lawyers and physicians and historians, and general scholars, but great engineers, physicists, chemists, and naturalists, — strong in developing the material resources of the nation. Nor have they done less for liberty than for civilization.

In a State whose central administration is thoroughly orthodox, and exercises strong political control, these universities are strongholds of freedom in politics and religion. In the halls of the University of Berlin, within a stone's-throw of the palace of the rigidly orthodox Frederick William IV., might be heard during his entire reign the free utterances of men opposed to every religious or political doctrine which the king thought essential. From the palace window, where the Emperor William loves to stand, can be seen in the university lecture-rooms, on the opposite side of the street, professors putting forth ideas fatal to absolute monarchy.

Bear in mind, too, that this is not the result of centuries of work, — a result impossible in a new country.

Though some of the German universities are on very old foundations, they have been remodelled to suit modern needs, and are in reality new: the greatest of all, the University of Berlin, is younger than the majority of our American colleges which have most reputation; and the greatest of her institutions for advanced instruction in the applied sciences have grown up within twenty years.

The result has been great, politically, intellectually, and morally. These universities, supported by the whole people, and for the whole people, stand far above any others in the world.

The United States, agreeing with Germany in the general line of her public school policy and primary education, has pursued an entirely different path in regard to university policy and advanced education.

While making primary and secondary education a matter of National and State concern, it has left its advanced education, in the main, to various religious sects. It has allowed an utterly illogical imaginary line to be drawn, below which the State provides for education gladly and fully, above which she turns the whole matter over to the sectarian spirit of the country. While the United States has pushed the roots of its public school system down into the needs and feelings of the whole people, and thus obtained a deep rich soil, which has given sturdy growth, it has pushed the roots of advanced education down into the multitude of scattered sects, and has obtained a soil wretchedly thin, and a growth miserably scant.

For the first result of this policy as to advanced education was, that, as sects multiplied, the so-called colleges and universities multiplied. Now, while the main condition of primary education is diffusion of resources, the main condition of advanced education is concentration of resources. England sees this, and has but four universities; imperial Prussia sees it, and has eight; the United States has not seen it, and the last Report of the Bureau of Education shows that we have over three hundred and sixty institutions bearing the name of "college" and "university."

The most evident result has been the impoverishment of the whole system. With very few exceptions, these colleges and universities are without any thing approaching complete faculties, without libraries giving any idea of the present condition of knowledge, without illustrative collections for study, without laboratories for experiment, with next to no modern apparatus and instruments. This is true of the whole country; but it is more sadly true of those States outside of the original thirteen.

The next striking result has been a lasting injury to those engaged in the work of advanced instruction. Many noble men stand in the faculties of those colleges and universities, — men who would do honor to any institution of advanced learning in the world. After much intercourse with university professors of various nations, I feel assured that I have never seen any who surpass in natural strength and earnestness very many in our own country; and I have heard this remarked more than once by thoughtful American fellow-students, while sitting in foreign university lecture-rooms. These men of ours would, under a better system, develop admirably the intellectual treasures of our people and the material resources of our country; but cramped by want of books, want of apparatus, want of every thing needed in advanced instruction, cramped, above all, by the spirit of the sectarian college system, very many of them have been paralyzed.

I know whereof I speak. Within the last twenty years I have seen much of these institutions, and within the last seven years I have made it a duty to watch them closely; and I freely confess that my observations have saddened me. Go from one great State to another, in every one you shall find that this unfortunate system has produced the same miserable results, — in the vast majority of our States not a single college or university worthy of the name; only a multitude of little sectarian schools with pompous names and poor equipments, each doing its best to prevent the establishment of any institution broader and better.

The traveller arriving in our great cities generally lands in a railway station costing more than all the university edifices of the State; and he sleeps in a hotel in which there is embarked more capital than in the entire university endowment for millions of people.

He visits asylums for lunatics, idiots, deaf, dumb, and blind, nay, even for the pauper and criminal, and he finds them palaces: he visits the college buildings for young men of sound mind and earnest purpose, the dearest treasures of the State, and he generally finds them in vile barracks. He inspects those asylums for men and women who are never more to be useful, and finds them provided with most perfect systems of ventilation: he visits the dormitories, recitation and lecture rooms, where live and move the young men who are to make or mar the State, and he finds them with systems of heating which vitiate the air, and with no ventilation. Examining still further, he finds that the inmates of the asylums have good food well prepared; he finds the inmates of colleges generally supplied with poor food badly prepared; he finds young men of sedentary and scholarly pursuits living in families where vinegar and grease are combined by the worst cookery in the world to form a diet which would destroy the stomachs of wood-choppers. Insufficient as intellectual training at most of these places is, the physical training is much worse, for it tends to make the great body of students sickly and weak and morbid, rather than strong pioneers of good thoughts, and sturdy bulwarks against political folly.

And, finally, there has come by the prevailing system a cramping of the intellectual development more unfortunate than that produced by poverty; for, as these institutions drew their nutriment mainly from sectarian effort, the controlling idea became sect growth, and not individual growth. As a result, each young man heard only professors of his own sect, or those affiliated with it. His philosophy, his history, his literature, was cast in the sect mould. The main result was not so much to educate the young man's mind as to warp it.

This was all the more natural because the various sects sometimes found their colleges convenient asylums for their unsatisfactory pastors, and their professorships comfortable shelves for men not successful in their pulpits. This was rendered all the more easy by the current superstition, that muddiness betokens depth, and that, if a clergyman be a dull preacher, he is probably a profound scholar. The result of this was, that the really strong men holding professorships were sometimes hampered by incompetent men, whose main function was to hear young men "parrot" text-books by rote in the recitation-room, and to denounce "science, falsely so called" in the chapel, varying these avocations by going around the country, denouncing every attempt at a better system as godless, and passing around the contribution-boxes in behalf of the bad system they represented.

Such is the main outline of the development of the American system of college instruction; and, if its result is in the main unsatisfactory, its present condition is mortifying.

This system of advanced education is now an old one. The time has arrived when it may be fully and fairly judged. It is not a new or young plant, as many fondly suppose: it has been developing more than two hundred years. By this time, if ever, we may expect a great, strong growth, a luxuriance in bloom and fruitage. But what do we see? Let me sum up with a few facts universally acknowledged. As to universities, our prevailing sect system has failed in two hundred and fifty years to develop one which ranks with institutions bearing that name in the other great civilized nations, some of them of far more recent creation than our own. The University of Berlin is younger than a multitude of our American colleges: it was brought up to its highest pinnacle by a nation crushed by military disaster and by financial burdens; yet no one will claim that we have an institution to compare with it.

As to schools of mechanical and

civil engineering, we are developing some which are doing excellent work; but we have not as yet one which will take rank with the multitude of such schools on the continent. To say nothing of such institutions as the French École Polytechnique, we have no advanced schools to compare with recent creations at Stuttgart, Carlsruhe, and Zurich.

As to laboratories, all these years of work in America, mainly shaped by the prevailing system, have failed to give us one to compare for a moment with several recently erected at Leipsic, Berlin, Heidelberg, Munich, and elsewhere, by government aid.

As to museums of the mechanic arts, all our collections combined would be as the small dust in the balance, when compared to the Conservatoire des Arts et Metiers.

As to art collections bearing on the various industries, if we were to add together all that our American system has accumulated, and multiply the sum by thousands, we should have nothing to approach the schools recently created by the English Government at South Kensington. As to various branches of instruction, we have many men in all departments equal to the best in Europe; but, for want of a university system to give scope to their ambition, they have almost entirely lacked opportunity. American students have been forced to pursue their most advanced studies abroad. Even as to that which is nearest us, — no full professorship of American history exists in our land. To study this history, young men have gone to sit at the feet of Laboulaye at Paris, Neumann at Berlin, and Kingsley at English Cambridge. It is in view of such a meagre growth in over two hundred years, under the prevailing system, that I present the following, as the fundamental proposition of this paper: —

The main provision for advanced education in the United States must be made by the people at large, acting through their National and State legislatures, to endow and maintain institutions for the higher instruction, fully equipped, and free from sectarian control.

And, first, I argue that *the past history and present condition of the higher education in the United States arouse a strong presumption in favor of making it a matter of public civil action, rather than leaving it to the prevailing system of private sectarian action.*

The history already given certainly arouses a presumption against the existing system; but that presumption is greatly strengthened by noticing what has been done, under the beginning of the plan I now advocate, — the plan under which the citizens of the various States of the United States have taken advanced education into their control.

Look briefly over this history of a better effort. The first good attempt to give to this country a true university, as distinguished from the American deterioration of the English college, was made by State action in the creation of the University of Virginia.

The prevailing sectarian system profited not at all by this example. The great universities of Germany grew into their modern state, nurseries of the love of learning and the love of freedom; but the sectarian college system of America went on multiplying the usual poor imitations of English colleges, when public civil action was again resorted to, and gave the beginning of another university: the combined bounty of the National and State Government, wisely administered, gave to the country the University of Michigan.

As to scientific and technological instruction, our country waited for years after such advanced instruction was given in Europe: but there came only scattered and feeble efforts; and the first great and comprehensive system which gave a college for applied science to every State in the Union was established by the congressional act of 1862, supplemented by the various acts of the State legislatures.

As to the illustration of natural science, the one collection in the United States that has acknowledged rank throughout the world is the one fostered by the wise and careful bounty of the State of Massachusetts at Cambridge.

And as to education in morals, that very education of what is best in man, which is claimed as the especial *raison d'être* of the prevailing sectarian system, the only institution which is generally recognized as strong enough to impress upon its whole teaching a sense of duty sufficiently deep to hold its own against the immoral tides of these times, the only one, which, when graduates of all other institutions fail, is, by common consent, appealed to, to give managers to our railways who will not plunder, investigators of our mines who will not lie, negotiators with our Indians who will not cheat, is the Government College at West Point.

But I argue next, that *careful public provision by the people for their own system of advanced instruction is the only republican and the only democratic method.*

While I hail with joy supplementary private gifts when not used as fetters, I maintain that there can be no system more unrepublican than that by which a nation or a state, in consideration of a few hundreds of thousands of dollars, delivers over its system of advanced instruction to be controlled and limited by the dogmas and whimseys of living donors or dead testators. In more than one nation, dead hands, stretching out from graves closed generations gone, have lain with a deadly chill upon institutions for advanced instruction during centuries. More than one institution in our own country has felt this grip and chill. The progress of civilization in the Old World since the French Revolution of 1789 has tended more and more to the building-up of its education in accordance with the needs of living men rather than the anticipations of dead men. My position is simply, that, if we ought to govern ourselves in any thing, we ought to govern ourselves in this; and that if, in matters of far less importance, we will not allow our rights, duties, and wants to be decided upon by this or that living man, we certainly ought not, in a matter of such vast importance as the higher education of our children, to allow our rights, duties, and wants to be decided upon by this or that dead man.

Again: I argue that *public provision, that is the decision and provision by each generation as to its own advanced education, is alone worthy of our dignity as citizens.*

What would be thought of a State which refused to build its State-house from its State treasury, and on the ostensible ground that private giving is good for the donor, and honorable to the State, begged individuals to build it? Should we not have a result exactly typical of what is exhibited in the prevailing system for advanced instruction? We should probably, if fortunate enough to get any thing at all, find, after a century, an edifice perfectly typical of what has been given us under our similar system in advanced education, — a Roman tower of brick here; a Gothic spire of stone there; a Greek pediment of wood here; a Renaissance cupola of iron there; a Doric column of porphyry next a Corinthian column of sandstone; no fitting approaches, because no one had given any thing so humble; halls too small, and doorways too narrow, and windows askew in accordance with this or that dead man's whimsey.

But this is the least. Suppose that we really get our building thus constructed, what would be thought of the policy which should leave the State building thus erected to be controlled forever, as to its occupancy and use, by living and dead donors, ancient and modern, and by their medley of ideas, religious and secular, forcible and feeble, crude and thoughtful, shrewd and absurd? And, if this system is incompatible with State and National dignity as regards a mere pile of stone and mortar, how much more so, when there is concerned the building of an edifice made of the best brains and hearts of living men, and the control of a great system of advanced education, in all its branches, for the entire nation, for all generations!

Again: I argue that *by public provision can private gifts be best stimulated.*

We have had in our country many noble examples of munificence toward institutions for advanced instruction; but no one thing seems to have stimulated them so much as the public endowments, which have aroused discussion, and afforded objects to which citizens of all creeds could contribute as a patriotic duty.

Take, as an example, the congressional grant of 1862, to national colleges, for scientific and industrial instruction. The recent reports of the United States Commissioner of Education show that gifts have been aggregated about these nuclei to the amount of over eight million dollars. Let me refer to an example within the State of New York. The national grant was concentrated upon one institution, the Cornell University. This encouraged thoughtful and liberal men to hope that something worthy of the State might be built upon that foundation; and the result is, that in eight years there have been added to that original endowment private gifts to the value of over a million, five hundred thousand dollars; and, so far as I can learn, none of these gifts would have been made but for the nucleus afforded by the national grant.

I argue next, that *by liberal public grants alone can our private endowments be wisely directed or economically aggregated.*

No one conversant with the history of advanced instruction in this country can have failed to note the ineffably absurd way in which large gifts for advanced instruction have been frittered away under the prevailing system.

There is hardly a State in the Union where the sums, large and small, that have been scattered among a multitude of petty sectarian institutions called colleges and universities, would not have produced one institution of great public value, had these gifts been directed to one object, and aggregated about one nucleus.

Compare two Western States lying near each other, — Ohio and Michigan. The State of Ohio has had every advantage over its northern neighbor as to population, soil, wealth, communication with the seaboard, and priority of complete occupation; but, as regards advanced education, it stumbled into the policy of scattered denominational colleges supported by sectarian beggary.

The State of Michigan took its national grant, developed upon that a State University; and from time to time its State legislature has added judiciously to it. Now look at the results. The great State of Ohio has within its borders not one college or university well equipped in any respect, — not one which rises above the third or fourth class. On the other hand, the State of Michigan has a noble university of the very first rank, with over a thousand students; and, what is of vast importance, the presence of such an institution has strengthened the whole system of public instruction throughout the State. No State has a more admirable series of primary schools and high schools; and her normal school ranks among the best, and so does her agricultural college. The system has been pronounced by thoughtful men from other States the best in the Union; and the whole secret of its excellence is, that, by wise and liberal legislation, stimulus and direction were given to private endowment. The difference between the two States I have named is, that in Michigan a public endowment gave statesmanlike direction to private endowment; while in Ohio all was frittered away and scattered between the clamors and intrigues of sects and localities.

So much for the direction of endowments: look now at their aggregation. Take the facts as they stand: I will mention cases well known. A weak denominational college in one of our States has received from a friend a great telescope worthy of the greatest institution in the world; but hardly any one else has given the institution any thing: there is no gift of a well-equipped observatory, or provision for an observer; and the telescope might as well be in Japan.

On the other hand, another denominational college has received the gift of a splendid observatory; but no one has added a gift of money for a telescope and other instruments. So the prevailing system gives you at one college a useless telescope, and at another a useless observatory.

I know of another denominational institution which has received a splendid geological collection; but as it has no provision for a geological laboratory, or for a geological professor, the collection, for all scientific purposes, is a mere illusion.

I know another denominational institution, which received from a denominational friend a splendid herbarium; but from the day it was received it has never been used, for the reason that no other member of the denomination has provided a professorship of botany.

I know another institution of this kind, which has received an excellent collection in mineralogy; but all appeals from the denomination to which it belongs have failed to secure an endowed professorship of metallurgy; and it would be money saved, had the collection never been taken out of the earth.

Compare this with the example I have just mentioned. The nation gave a moderate grant for a university to the State of Michigan: the State legislature added to it judiciously. Thus was built up one great institution. The result is, that from various parts of the State, and from other States, gifts have been aggregated about the nucleus thus formed. Thus was provided both a telescope and an observatory; thus has its library been enlarged; thus were developed its illustrative collections. They are a matter of State concern and State pride; and individual gifts come in from all sides more and more to supplant public gifts.

The same, in a less degree, may be seen in several other universities: the only difficulty in these cases is, that public gifts have been too small to give the public system a fair and full trial.

But I argue next, that *our existing public school system leads logically and necessarily to the endowment of advanced instruction.*

For years the prevalent American practice has divorced the primary and secondary education from advanced education. Never was a system more illogical; never did a system more fully show its unreason by its results.

When we attempt to divorce advanced from preliminary education, we are simply persisting in cutting the whole mass of branches and boughs and blossoms of education from the trunk; and when we succeed in rearing goodly trees by persistently sawing off all their upper growth, and leaving the bare trunk, then, and not till then, can we have goodly systems of primary and secondary public schools, while we cut off from them the whole development of higher education.

Again I cite the State of Michigan. Its university, in which its whole system of public instruction culminates, has shed light and life into its high schools, and those again into the great number of secondary and primary schools. The best graduates are constantly going into the teacherships of the high schools, and their best pupils into charge of the primary schools. These last, in their turn, send up their best men through intermediate grades to the university. The result is a system of which the whole State is becoming proud, and one which puts to shame the feeble anarchy prevailing in the education of most of her sister States.

If there should be public provision for any education at all, it should be a good provision; and there can be no good provision for any part of a system of public instruction which does not develop every part fully, and all parts harmoniously. To be a good system, it must be a living system; and it cannot be a living system, unless its growth be complete. If its highest parts are left to wither, its trunk and roots will wither also.

Again: I argue that *the existing system of public endowments for advanced education in matters relating to the military and naval service leads logically to public provision for advanced education in matters relating to the civil service of the nation.*

If the preservation of the national honor is the ground for public provision in one case, it is the ground in the other. Nay, if the preservation of the national existence is the ground in one case, it is the ground not less in the other. The number in military and naval service is less than twenty thousand: the number of those in civil service, counting National and State officials, is probably ten times that number.

See where the hap-hazard system of public advanced education, doled out to a great nation by various sects, has led us. From one end of the country to the other there is not a regular permanent provision for advanced instruction in the history of the United States. Look the whole number of three hundred and sixty colleges through, and you do not find, save in one or two, any regular provision for instruction in political economy and social science. Take the plainest results as regards social science. Every year the cost is fearful. Nearly forty State legislatures, and nearly forty times forty county and local boards, dealing with matters relating to pauperism, crime, lunacy, idiocy, the care of the deaf, dumb, and blind, making provision regarding them at a cost of millions upon millions, and very rarely with any fundamental study of the complicated questions involved. Yonder is England suffering from errors in these respects made centuries ago: here are our States repeating many of the same errors.

Take next the simple results as regards political science. Look at our national legislature, containing always a large number of strong men and patriotic men, but the strongest of them often given up to theories which the most careful thinking of the world, and the world's experience as recorded in history, long since exploded.

But the analogy extends beyond the internal affairs of our Nation and States: it extends to our external relations. I do not speak of the diplomatic service, though the want of higher knowledge with reference to that has long been felt; but I allude to an analogy of another sort forced upon us by these times.

I start again with the premises universally conceded, that public provision is necessary to fit men to take part in warfare by land and sea, to hold our country in the position she ought to occupy among modern nations.

But the warfare to which men are educated at West Point and Annapolis is not the only warfare between modern States.

The greatest modern warfare is rapidly becoming an industrial warfare. Every great nation is recognizing this. But the most striking thing about it is a change in methods. The old system of waging war by tariffs and bounties is yielding to the system of developing national taste and skill by *technical education.* That is the meaning of the great expositions of industry of the last twenty-five years: that is the meaning of all the great institutions which modern States are providing for higher education in the sciences bearing upon the various industries, — education to enable nations to hold their own among modern States, — education in civil, mining, and mechanical engineering; in the application of the natural and physical sciences to agriculture and manufacture; in arts of design as applied to the making of various fabrics.

This warfare is real as the other. The army engaged in it is larger than in the other: it is on our side eight million strong; and the nation which leaves education regarding it to the driblets which can be wheedled out of individuals by sectarian appeals will find that it has neglected its highest duties, and abdicated some of its noblest functions.

Again: I argue that *not only does a true regard for the material prosperity of the nation demand a more regular and thorough public provision for advanced education, but that our highest political interests demand it.*

From all sides come outcries against the debasement of American politics, and especially against gross material corruption. No doubt, great part of these cries are stimulated by scandal-hunters and sensation-mongers; still enough remains to give much food for serious thought.

Now, I assert, that, as a rule, our public men who have received an advanced education have not yielded to gross corruption. Understand the assertion. It is not that men who have not had the advantages of an advanced education yield generally to corrupt influences, — far from it; some of the noblest opponents of corruption we have had have been men debarred by early poverty from thorough education, — but what I assert is simply this: go among the men who disgrace our country by gross corruption, — whether in city, state, or national councils, — and you find the great majority of them of the class that has received just education enough to enter into the struggle for place or pelf, and not enough to appreciate higher considerations.

The preliminary education which many of our strongest men have received leaves them simply beasts of prey: it has simply sharpened their claws, and whetted their tusks. But a higher education, whether in science, literature, or history, not only sharpens a man's faculties, but gives him new exemplars and ideals. His struggle for place and pelf is, as a rule, modified by considerations to which a man of lower education is very often a stranger. He is lifted up to a plane from which he can look down upon success in corruption with the scorn it deserves. The letting-down in character of our National and State councils has notoriously increased, just as the predominance of men of advanced education in those councils has decreased. President Barnard's admirable paper, showing the relatively diminishing number of men of advanced education in our public stations, decade by decade, marks no less the rise, decade by decade, of material corruption. This is not mere concomitancy: there is a relation here of cause and effect.

If we are to have more statesmen of that high type which is alone worthy of a republic, we must have better provision for educating the young men of rude strength, who are taking hold of public affairs in all parts of our country, and especially in the great States of the West. We must have an education provided for, that shall lift them above mere mammon-worship, into those realms where the great thoughts of great men give the atmosphere in which can best be cultivated a sense of duty to God and to country. To give better men to public stations, you must have provisions for instructing our strongest young men, which shall lift them above the prevalent idea of life among such multitudes of our successful men, — the idea that life is a game of grasping and griping for forty years, with a whine for God's mercy at the end of it.

And, finally, I insist that *it is a duty of society to itself, a duty which it cannot throw off, to see that the stock of talent and genius in each generation have chance for development, that it may be added to the world's stock, and aid in the world's work.*

Of all State treasures, the genius and talent of citizens are the most precious. That arch Bohemian, Sala, said that in no country is there so much genius and talent "lying around loose" as in America. Now, it is just this genius and talent, which, as all history shows, private capacity, and the law of supply and demand, will not develop.

But I am met here, first, by an undue extension of the *laissez faire* argument. It is said that the best policy is to leave the building-up of such institutions entirely to private hands; that such a plan educates the people to give, makes them self-reliant.

The latest form of this argument was put forth in the National Association of Teachers last year at Elmira, in a speech by President Eliot of Harvard.

Now, I do not yet take up the question of a single national university at the national capital; but when the distinguished president of Harvard College condemns by implication, as in the speech to which I have referred, all public provision for advanced instruction, whether by Nation or State, we all have the right to stand amazed. At its very beginning, the university over which he presides had aid from the State in which it stands; and it has not been slow to accept public aid at various periods since. In these latter days, its greatest glory, its museum of natural science, is largely the result of constant application to the legislature of Massachusetts. The whole country has rejoiced that the State of Massachusetts has had the practical good sense thus to grant funds to carry on the great work of Prof. Agassiz at Harvard; and they rejoiced also when the liberality of the State stimulated a noble growth of private liberality.

But this is not all. So far as the public has learned, there stands in the annals of that university no record of any rejection of favors, even from the National Government. The benefits accruing to that institution from the Coast Survey are well known; and when rich spoils came to it from the dredging expedition of "The Hassler," a national ship, I remember no Spartan voice raised to repel them.

But grant that the argument against public aid is good at Harvard, is it good anywhere else in this country? It certainly cannot be held good at Yale, or at Dartmouth, or at Brown, or at Rutgers, or at the University of Vermont, — institutions which received the national grant of 1862 for promoting the application of science to industry, and are making a most noble return for the gift.

Grant that Harvard can now dispense with public aid (although her recent history looks so little like it), it does not at all follow that the other institutions of the country can dispense with it. Close under the shadow of the great palaces and warehouses of a metropolitan city, that institution, to the joy of us all, is the recipient of splendid gifts from princely merchants and scholars. But how few of our colleges have the advantage of being near so great an accumulation of capital!

Nor is this all. Harvard can afford to speak complacently to her young sisters, for she is enjoying the accumulations of two hundred years. But are the Western States to wait two hundred years? Here is the whole question. The prospect held out to the younger States is, that those of their colleges which happen to be near great centres of wealth may, in a century or two, arrive at the position which Harvard has now attained.

But I come to the second part of the objection: Is it necessary that public provision be withheld in order that private persons may give, and that public spirit may thus be cultivated? Even if it be so, I fail to see force in the argument. As well might President Eliot argue against any public provision for policemen, in order that individuals may toughen their muscles in fighting ruffians; or against any public provision for prisons, in order that individuals may sharpen their minds in outwitting thieves. The history of the private gifts for education, crystallized about the various public gifts, and especially about that of 1862, shows that well-directed public bounty stimulates private bounty. It shows that Americans will give where they see something well established to which it seems worth while to give. "To him that hath shall be given" is the rule for advanced education.

The *laissez faire* argument is good against government provision for those things which private persons may be fairly expected to establish and maintain from expectation of gain; but all history shows that advanced education is not one of those things. The greatest modern apostle of the *laissez faire* principle, John Stuart Mill, on this and other grounds, especially excludes education in all its grades from the operation of the *laissez faire* principle. Says Mr. Mill, —

"But there are other things of the worth of which the demand of the market is by no means a test, — things of which the utility does not consist in ministering to inclinations, nor in serving the daily uses of life, and the want of which is least felt where the need is greatest. This is peculiarly true of those things which are chiefly useful as tending to raise the character of human beings. . . . It will continually happen on the voluntary system, that, the end not being desired, the means will not be provided at all, or that, the persons requiring improvement having an imperfect or altogether erroneous conception of what they want, the supply called forth by the demand of the market will be any thing but what is really required. . . . Education, therefore, is one of those things which it is admissible in principle that a government should provide for the people. The case is one to which the reasons of the non-interference principle do not necessarily or universally extend."

And again: —

"In the matter of education, the intervention of government is justifiable, because the case is not one in which the interest and judgment of the consumer are a sufficient security for the goodness of the commodity." [1]

But it is said that universities publicly endowed would overshadow the existing colleges. Doubtless this would be the case with many of the weakest ones in the newer States; but is that a hardship? If there is any thing in the matter of education for which Michigan and California and Wisconsin and Minnesota have reason to bless their early statesmen, it is just this creation of State universities, which have overshadowed the whole corps of little sectarian colleges and universities, or rather rendered them impossible.

But while the whole brood of feeble colleges must thus be weakened, I firmly believe that the really strong colleges and universities, even those which have grown up under the old system, would be greatly strengthened thereby. This is not mere theory. Look at the history of advanced instruction during the last ten years. Several of our older institutions were, ten years ago, in a state of torpor, or of very moderate progress, to say the least. What was the beginning of a new order of things at Harvard? Notoriously the famous pamphlet of Dr. Hedge, exhibiting the system and work of the University of Michigan. From that publicly-endowed institution in the West came a very strong impulse to university-growth in the East. The interest in university progress at Harvard and Yale, and Wesleyan and Amherst, and Prince-

[1] Mill, Political Economy, vol. ii. book v.

ten and Union, and Lafayette and Washington-Lee Colleges, has unquestionably been aided by the spirit thus aroused. What is wanted in this country is examples which will stamp into the mind of our people what a true university ought to be. Show an example of this sort to the friends of the really strong old colleges, so that they can really understand it, and they will give liberally to build up their older colleges as nobly as any new ones. Let any State develop its university never so high, the alumni of Harvard and Yale, and Columbia and Brown, and Princeton and Union and Rutgers, and others of like vigor, will not let their own colleges be behindhand.

Still another argument in opposition runs as follows: "No institution can be Christian, unless there be some denominational dogma as its basis; a publicly-endowed institution cannot accept any denominational basis: therefore it will be infidel and atheistic;" or, to put it in shorter form, "a college must be sectarian to be Christian."

To say nothing of other difficulties, one fatal difficulty with this argument is, that it proves too much. As Bishop McQuaid of Rochester recently urged with great cogency, this argument, if good for any thing against institutions of advanced instruction, is far stronger against our whole common-school system. The simplest view of the subject shows us that there is far more reason for requiring sectarian schools for children, who cannot provide for their own religious wants, and who are at the most tender and impressible period, than for young men, whose fundamental ideas are already formed, to a great extent, and who have free access to multitudes of devoted clergymen, and to the Christian associations and churches, and to the other good appliances accessible in a Christian country.

But it is said, "Your legislatures and public authorities will manage such trusts badly, and appoint unfit persons to professorships."

Some will do so at first; most will not. Save in one or two cases, no such charge can be made in the whole history of State management of over forty State universities and colleges, and a still greater number of normal schools.

Nor can this charge be made against the management by the United States of the national academies at West-Point and Annapolis, or of the Smithsonian Institution, under the very eaves of the national Capitol.

Favoritism and mismanagement are likely to be far greater in the close corporations of denominational colleges, each too weak to live without propitiating the "leading men of the denomination."

But it is said, "The denominational colleges have given to the country many strong men." True; but what does this prove? Extend the argument a little. A simple printing-office education has given to the country many strong men, — such men as Franklin and Greeley; but does it follow that we should have no other agency for developing the latent talent and genius of the country?

The colleges have developed much talent for the pulpit, bar, and forum; but we need yet stronger agencies for developing yet more; and the proof is to be found in Dr. Barnard's statistics, which show the declining number, proportionately, of college-bred men in all our public positions, executive, legislative, and judicial.

Besides this, our needs are vastly increased and extended. Our modern civilization demands now what very few of our colleges and universities are prepared to give, — thorough training in civil, mechanical, and mining engineering, in architecture, in chemistry applied to agriculture and manufactures, in all those sciences and arts which are building modern civilization. The little college with four or five professors is no longer enough. To meet this modern need, we want institutions most thoroughly and largely equipped with laboratories, libraries, museums, experimental grounds, observatories, and the like, which demand great concentration of means in a few places.

But it is said, "Institutions for advanced instruction are for the wealthy, for rich men's sons, and not for the poor."

Nothing could be more wide of the fact. The rich man is indeed vastly interested indirectly; for thorough provision for advanced education will raise up a thoughtful class of men, who are the natural enemies of all the wild theories which tend to desolate society, or disturb public prosperity; but, if any person more than another is fully and directly interested, it is the poor man. The rich man can send his son to another State or to another country; the poor man cannot. The doctrine I advocate is the only one, which, in many parts of our country, can insure a worthy education to the sons of poor men. The whole experience of the world shows, that from the ranks of poverty comes by far the greatest part of the genius and talent and energy of the world. In the great majority of our States, this great class, disciplined by poverty, have no chance for any advanced education in applied science, in civil engineering, in mechanical engineering, in mining engineering, and kindred departments, and very little chance in any other, unless there be public endowments for advanced instruction.

And now what should our practical policy be in carrying out the general principle I have advocated? Let us see if we cannot get out of the realm of theory into the realm of practice.

And first, as to *practical dealings with the question in the newer States.* Now, there is one very fortunate thing in the whole matter; and that is, as regards public provision for education in the new States, there is already a National and State policy, based on the right principle, and tending to the right direction. It has not been carried out with sufficient liberality or continuity; still it has always been in one direction, and that is, I think, the right direction. In accordance with this policy, the Congress of the United States gave the newer States, —

First, a grant of land to serve as a nucleus fund for primary and secondary instruction.

Second, Congress gave the States a grant to serve as a nucleus fund for university instruction.

Third, Congress has given to the new States, as well as to the old, a grant to serve as a nucleus fund for instruction, especially in sciences bearing on the great industries. This National and State policy, thus in harmony, has begun to be supplemented by an individual policy. Already individuals are beginning to aggregate gifts about the funds thus provided by the Nation and the State.

Here, then, is a policy distinct and consistent. So far as it has been carried out, it has worked well. The only difficulty is, that it has been carried out too slowly and timidly: what I advocate is, that it be carried out firmly and logically. I would have Congress strengthen the foundations it has laid in the States, thoughtfully and liberally, in view of the vast populations that are to reside in those States, and in view of the absolute necessity of having strong centres of enlightenment in those vast populations.

Next, as to State policy. I would have it go in the same direction as heretofore, but with a liberality and steadiness showing far more foresight. I would have each of those States build up higher upon the foundations laid by national grants their public institutions for advanced instruction as distinguished from private sectarian institutions. I would have each State build up the one institution under its control, rather than the twenty under the control of conferences and dioceses and synods and councils and consistories and presbyteries, and denominational associations of various sects. I would have Michigan develop more completely her excellent normal school at Ypsilanti, and her agricultural college at Lansing, and add a department of technology, and a mining school, to her noble university at Ann Arbor. I would have Illinois strengthen her admirable industrial university at Champaign; and Arkansas, hers at Lafayette. I would have Missouri strengthen her State university at Columbia, and her mining school at Rolla; and Iowa strengthen her State college at Ames; and Minnesota, her State university at St. Anthony; and California go on, as she recently has done so liberally, and strengthen her university at Berkeley; and Kentucky, hers at Ashland; and so with the rest.

This is a policy which may be groaned over or sighed at by those whose whole system of public action consists, not in promoting a practicable plan, but in groaning over and scolding at every thing supposed to contravene ultra doctrines of non-interference and the ultra *laissez faire* phrases; but it is a policy already adopted, and is the only one which can give advanced education to our great new States.

Let me sum up the whole case based on facts presented in public reports, which I ask you as thoughtful men to ponder. Remember, then, that in not one of our States, outside the original thirteen, has there yet been established by private enterprise or sectarian zeal a college or university with a faculty approaching completeness as to numbers, or with a general equipment which reaches mediocrity. In the whole number of such sectarian institutions, there is not one complete faculty, not one library, laboratory, observatory, or illustrative collection, worthy of even the third rank, even judging by our American standard. This is the outcome of nearly a century of effort, under the principle of scattering resources for advanced education in accordance with the demands of sectarianism, rather than concentrating them in accordance with the plans of statesmanship.

So much for the great new States.

Turn now to the older States. What should be our policy with them? Wise statesmanship dictates that we be not fettered by a single theory or doctrine, no matter how good in the abstract. The older States, having had more time for developing institutions for advanced instruction, and not having scattered resources with utter prodigality as the new States have done, have built up a small number of colleges and universities of real strength. On their foundation I would have public grants and private gifts combined. Here, too, fortunately, there is a well-defined National policy, and, to some extent, a State policy.

The National Government acted in accordance with it when it gave the grant of lands for general and scientific and industrial education in 1862; and the States acted in accordance with it, when they appropriated that grant, — Connecticut to Yale, New Hampshire to Dartmouth, Vermont to the Vermont University, New Jersey to Rutgers, Massachusetts to the State Agricultural College and Institute of Technology, Rhode Island to Brown University. The Scripture rule in this case is, "to him that hath shall be given;" the scientific rule is, let there be a "survival of the fittest;" and the plain rule of common-sense — whether in nation or State, whether in old States or new, whether for public or private gifts — is, for primary education, diffusion; for advanced education, concentration of resources.

And, as to the general application of these rules, the history of all civilized nations, and especially our own, shows that the thoughtful statesmanship of each generation should provide for the primary, secondary, and advanced education of each generation.

Accepting this principle, the immediate care should evidently be to strengthen by public action the best foundations for advanced education which we already have; and although I am not here as the advocate of a single national university, yet I may say, that should the National Government take a few of the strongest in various parts of the country, and, by greater endowments still, make them national universities; or should it create one or more new ones worthy of the nation, placing one of them at the national capital, where the vast libraries, museums, and laboratories of various sorts now existing may be made of use for advanced instruction, and where the university could act directly and powerfully for good in sending graduates admirably prepared into the very heart and centre of our national civil service, to elevate and strengthen it, — I believe, in spite of pessimists and doctrinaires, that the result would tell for good upon the whole country.

I do not enter into details of any particular plan: for this I refer you to the thoughtful papers of Prof. Hoyt and Senator Howe. My aim has been simply to lay down and illustrate the great principles which must serve as a foundation in this whole matter.

And now a word in answer to the objections recently put forth by Dr. McCosh.

The doctor first objects to the term "sectarian college," and asks what I mean by it. I can easily answer him. A sectarian college is a college controlled by any single sect, or combination of sects. Sometimes this control is exercised by giving the favored sect a majority of trustees or professors; sometimes by requiring the president to be a clergyman of a peculiar sect; sometimes by organizing the controlling body, at the beginning, in the interest of the sect, and then keeping it a close corporation. Unfortunately, the answer to the learned doctor's question is written over the whole history of American education, and in letters very big and black. From the days when Henry Dunster, the first president of Harvard College, a devoted scholar, and earnest man, was driven from his seat with ignominy and cruelty, because, as Cotton Mather said afterwards, he had "fallen into the briars of anti-pedobaptism," the sectarian spirit has been the worst foe of advanced education.

But, if the doctor thinks examples of this sort too old, I will point him to some well known in our time. One of the most honored college presidents of New York was driven out of his professorship of natural philosophy in a New-England college because he was an Episcopalian. One of the most honored college presidents of New England was driven away from a professorship of Greek in a New-York college because he was a Unitarian. One of the most renowned college presidents in the Western States was excluded from a professorship in the State of New York because he was a Presbyterian. One of the main university presidencies in New England remained in these latter years vacant for a long time. Why? There were scholars, jurists, statesmen, in that Commonwealth, who would have done honor to the position. Why were they not called? Simply because the statute of the university required the presiding officer to be a Baptist. One of the most important colleges in the State of New York rejected one of the best modern chemists because he was not of the required sect: a noted college in a neighboring State rejected one of our most noted astronomers and mathematicians for the same reason. Nay, within a few years I have had personal knowledge, as a trustee of the college concerned, of the following case: a college had suffered long for want of a professor of rhetoric and English literature, upon a foundation already endowed. A man of the required sect was at last found admirably fitted; but this man was rejected. Why? Simply because he was not of a particular party in that particular sect. Does the doctor wish to know what an unsectarian university is? I point him to the charter given by the State of New York to the university which I have the honor to serve. It contains the following clauses: "Persons of any religious sect, or of no religious sect, shall be equally eligible to all offices and appointments." And again, "No person shall be accepted or rejected as trustee, professor, or student, on account of any religious or political views which he may or may not entertain."

But Dr. McCosh praises Yale College, and asks whether I consider that a sectarian college. Let me say here to the doctor, that, while I may be willing to sit at his feet to learn some other duties, I cannot acknowledge him as my instructor regarding my filial duty to my *Alma Mater*. Among all her sons, no one loves her or respects her more than I; and my love and respect for her grow with the years, because I see that she is nobly working out of the sectarian fetters which her early history threw about her. She has appointed several men to professorships without compelling them to submit to any tests of orthodoxy whatever. In her faculty may to-day be found men utterly at variance with the theology which she has been supposed to represent.

She has never lost her presence of mind in view of Darwinism; nor has she ever allowed a scientific professorship to remain vacant for fear that she might find in her faculty a believer in evolution.

The doctor expressed fear that

trouble might arise from difference in belief among professors, and thought some one religious body must be in control. To show how little he understands the problem as it has been wrought out in this country, I can point him to the University of Virginia, the University of Michigan, the Cornell University, the Industrial University of Illinois, the normal schools and national colleges in the various States, which have gone on perfectly easily and smoothly under the system I advocate, and with infinitely less of religious quarrelling than has taken place in several colleges under the guidance of a particular sect.

Again: the doctor objects to any dependence upon State and National aid, because, he says, their officers would be obliged to present their cases to the State legislature, and there would be "lobbying;" and he draws a picture of the wretchedness arising from university officers taking part in this business. But there is another picture far more wretched: it is the picture of college presidents and professors inflicting themselves *ad nauseam* upon the pulpits and parlors of their particular denomination "to present the claims" of their special sectarian college; the picture of college officials paying court at the tables of rich members of the sect to catch some drippings for their respective colleges; the picture of professors of colleges driven to watch for legacies at the hands of aged widows and spinsters. This is a picture infinitely more sad than that of the college officer as a citizen presenting the claims of advanced education to the Educational Committee of the legislature, or to its various members, and enforcing upon them the duty that the State owes in the education of its citizens. And, finally, the doctor gained some applause, apparently from undergraduates collected in the hall when he spoke, by the assertion that American colleges and universities send out graduates as well prepared as do the great foreign universities. The doctor possibly mistakes me. I made no reference to the smaller queen's colleges of Ireland. If he says that the scholarship of their students at graduation is lower than that in our American colleges, I shall take his word for it, and pity Ireland all the more. But if he meant that our American universities, any of them, graduate men on an equality, as regards scholarship, with the great universities of the Old World, I will not put assertion against assertion, though my experience among those universities at home and abroad as a student (I state it simply as a matter of fact) is greater than his own, but I will simply point to facts which utterly disprove his assertion. If his assertion be true, why is it that a stream of the foremost scholars of our foremost universities sets steadily toward the great universities of the Old World? Why do our best graduates of Harvard, Yale, Michigan, Princeton, Wesleyan, Cornell, and Columbia, and all the rest, constantly go abroad to perfect themselves in these same studies? Why was it that the late presidents of Harvard and Yale, and their present presidents, both pursued their studies abroad after graduation at home? Why is it that almost every professor of note in our leading colleges, in every important department, has perfected his studies abroad after graduating at home? To provoke the applause of undergraduates, Dr. McCosh's assertion was good enough, and he appears to have learned early how to minister to the American appetite for praise; but as a statement soberly made before a body anxious to get at the truth of the matter, and to do something to help on advanced education in the country, the statement seems to be utterly unworthy.

And one more question may be asked, What shall be done with this great multitude of denominational colleges already existing? I answer to that, Let them become intermediate colleges, holding a place like that of the great English schools or the German gymnasia, between the lower preparatory schools and the universities. As such they could render a vast service to the country.

There would be no lessening in their dignity, or in the position of those who manage them. Our mother-country gives her highest honors to those intermediate colleges, and to those who govern them. Eton and Harrow and Rugby are places of pilgrimage; and that galaxy in which Hawtrey and Arnold and Temple stood is one of the glories of our race. Nor is our own country without examples. Any president of college or university might prize the fame of Taylor of Andover.

And now, in closing, let me present the two practical conclusions from my argument: —

First, In the older States public and private aid should be concentrated upon a small number of the broadest and strongest foundations already laid.

Second, In the newer States, State aid should be regularly and liberally given to State institutions, for the highest literary, scientific, and industrial instruction, to fully equip them, and to keep them free from sectarian control.

EDWARD E. HALE,
Editor.

ROBERTS BROS.
Publishers,

THE PEOPLE'S MAGAZINE.

A new Series of this Monthly will begin in January, 1875, with the Eleventh Volume.

The department of FINE ART, which has especially attracted Amateur Artists, will be placed under the charge of two distinguished artists of Boston.

The department called the RECORD OF PROGRESS, which is a chronicle of the latest improvements in social order, is under the editorial charge of F. B. SANBORN, the Secretary of the Social Science Association.*

The EXAMINER is an impartial Review of the most important books published in England, France, Germany, and America. It is under the special oversight of FREDERIC B. PERKINS.

The editorial charge of the literary, political, and speculative departments remains with EDWARD E. HALE.

OLD AND NEW has won its wide circulation by its popular stories, from the pens of Mrs. Stowe, Mrs. Whitney, Bishop Clark, Geo. Mac Donald, Miss Meredith, Miss Hale, Mrs. Julia Ward Howe, Mr. Burnand, Mr. Perkins, Mr. Hale, Mr. Trollope, and other popular writers. These stories, short and long, form a prominent part of the magazine.

Our SKETCHING CLUB, by REV. ST. JOHN TYRWHITT has special value for young artists just beginning to draw from nature.

The MUSICAL REVIEW is a safe guide to all purchasers of Music who are far from the Music Shops.

The invaluable series of articles on social, political, and religious reform which have been contributed by Dr. Leonard Bacon, Mr. Theodore Bacon, Hon. Andrew D. White, Rev. H. W. Bellows, Fred. B. Sanborn, John E. Williams, Rowland S. Hazard, and other writers of distinction, will be regularly continued.

REV. DR. MARTINEAU'S Essays will be completed in this volume.

Subscription price of "Old and New" $4.00 a Year.

(To Clergymen at Trade Price.)

Address

F. B. PERKINS, Business Agent.

143 Washington Street, ... Boston.

OLD AND NEW.

The Peoples' Magazine.

Edited by EDWARD E. HALE.

AUTUMN CAMPAIGN.

Three Months Free! Binding Covers Free!

ALL NEW ANNUAL SUBSCRIBERS to Old and New for 1875, who send their subscription previous to Dec. 1st, 1874, will receive the October, November and December numbers of 1874 FREE, or if preferred can have their subscription commence with the October 1874 number, and have the July, August and September 1874 numbers FREE, thus obtaining the commencement of the present Volume. All present subscribers to Old and New who RENEW their subscriptions previous to December 1st, 1874, will receive Binding Covers for any two of the volumes of the Old and New already issued, which they may prefer.

This offer for both Old and New subscribers holds good to Dec. 1st, 1874, and NO LATER. Also no other premiums or inducements will be offered.

Terms---Only $4.00 a Year.

(To Clergymen at Trade Price.)

Specimen Copies of latest issue sent postpaid on receipt of 35 cents.

All communications relating to the Business, Subscriptions, Advertisements, &c., should be addressed to

F. B. PERKINS, Business Agent,

OFFICE OLD AND NEW,

143 Washington St., Boston, Mass.

www.ingramcontent.com/pod-product-compliance
Lightning Source LLC
LaVergne TN
LVHW011143110826
845150LV00008B/2479

* 9 7 8 1 4 1 8 1 9 2 2 3 5 *